I0150947

Shards of Blue

poems by

Michael Ratcliffe

Finishing Line Press
Georgetown, Kentucky

Shards of Blue

ACKNOWLEDGMENTS

The following poems appeared previously in *The Copperfield Review*, some in
slightly different versions:

John's Lament
Separated in Life, Even As In Death
She Will Not Thirst Again
The Glass
The Mountains Were My Meetinghouse
The Wheat Field
When Fremont Left the Farm

Editor: Christen Kincaid

Cover Art: Laura K. Ryan

Author Photo: Brian K. Donnelly Photography

Cover Design: Elizabeth Maines

Printed in the USA on acid-free paper.
Order online: www.finishinglinepress.com
also available on amazon.com

Author inquiries and mail orders:
Finishing Line Press
P. O. Box 1626
Georgetown, Kentucky 40324
U. S. A.

Table of Contents

These poems are dedicated to the memory of my great-great grandparents,
John Ratcliff and Mary Townsend Ratcliff. This is their story.

SEPARATED IN DEATH, EVEN AS IN LIFE

Separated in death,
even as in life—
her seven sons laid her to rest
in a new grave,
moved from the farm
to what became the family plot
when he died—
John at one end,
Mary at the other,
and between them a space
as wide as the schism in their lives.

What were the sons thinking
when they buried their father
and reburied their mother?
Why did they move her
from the farm she plowed
out of the dry Kansas soil?
Did they envision them all together again
embraced by mother and father?

Or, did they keep them separate
out of respect for her,
with themselves someday
shielding her in death
from the disappointment
and hurt that he caused?

In the end, the sons are scattered—
all the generations scattered—
and in the family plot
only a few remained to fill
the space between the graves.

So lie John and Mary:
separated in death, even as in life,
and nothing carved upon their stones
to tell us they were once together.

A DIFFERENT KIND OF QUAKER

John Ratcliff, from the Ohio Town Company settlement,
Marshall County, Kansas, 1855

Dear Mary,
I don't know when this letter might reach you,
but I want you to know that I am well.
I miss you and the boys.
There is much work to keep me busy,
but still I find myself stopping at times
to think about what you might be doing.
Nights feel so long without you next to me.

The journey to Kansas passed without event,
though the riverboats down the Ohio
and up the Missouri were crowded and hot.
Westport was boisterous with activity—
migrants stocking up for the trails
to Oregon and California,
Mormons bound for Salt Lake,
and Free-Soilers like us,
all armed and setting out for Kansas.
We bought our supplies
and headed for our claims.

We measured out the boundaries
of the town, marked the corners of our farms.
Pro-slavery men are already here—
South Carolinians in Palmetto,
Missourians in Marysville—
but they seem peaceful enough.
Still, we are on our guard
and take turns patrolling day and night.
Oh, if the Elders in Mt. Pleasant could see us—
we carry guns at all times.
We decided we will fight if it comes to that.
Kansas calls for a different kind of Quaker.

I WAS MADE FOR THIS LAND
John, 1856

End of day.
The field is plowed and ready for planting.
Beyond, the tall grass flows toward the westering sky.
The setting sun casts its light in orange and red across the prairie.
In the East, night has fallen; shadows move across the land.

I work this land to the rhythms of the day—
the morning and the evening sun, the sun at noon.
In Wheeling, the glassworks' clock ruled my day—
when to rise and when to quit.
On First Days, the Elders watched and queried.
On this prairie I am my guide;
I preside over my life and my thoughts.
I was made for this land.

THE MOUNTAINS WERE MY MEETINGHOUSE
Mary Townsend Ratcliff, 1856

The mountains were my meetinghouse;
solace found among the silent groves
of hemlock and rhododendra
and mountain laurel.
Botany my religion; worship in Latin,
names repeated as liturgy:
Tsuga canadiensis
Rhododendra vaseyi
Kalmia latifolia.

The mountains were my meetinghouse;
friends met in meadows and forest glades.
I knew them all by name:
trillium, teaberry, bee balm,
goldenrod, primrose,
and forget-me-nots,
oh, how I loved
their blue flowers in May.

On this prairie, so much that's unfamiliar.
I know I'll learn the names some day,
but for now I am lost
in a tall-grass sea of doubt
wondering what will be my meetinghouse?
How will I ground my faith
that we were right to move
to this prairie,
so far from all we've known?

In time I'll learn to name the plants.
In time I'll learn to love this land.

LIFE ON THE PRAIRIE SUITS US
Mary, 1857

Dear Cousin,
We received with warmth and gladness
your letter of November last. How nice
to receive news from Ohio of family
and to learn that all are in good health.
We are thriving; life on the prairie suits us.
Work on the farm keeps us busy.
John and I have found we work well together.
The boys are healthy and strong.
Gene has grown so big—
I call him my tall-grass son.
He helps look after young John,
who began walking last summer.

Though the prairie is beautiful
I do miss the hills and mountains,
and even the bustle and clamor of Wheeling.
If you think of it, could you send
pressed flowers to remind me of home?

You asked whether we are safe.
I am pleased to report that the violence
that has stricken parts of this Territory
has not been seen in our vicinity.
For now, Pro-Slavery and Free-Soiler
live peaceably together in this county.
We pray that violence will not reach us.
But, I must admit, we do not put
all our trust in God. Each household
keeps rifles ready. Even I have learned to shoot.

WHAT WONDERFUL DAYS THESE ARE
Mary, Spring 1862

Spring has returned to the prairie.
The sky is a beautiful cornflower blue,
the air still more cool than hot.

John plows furrows in the field
like he's etching lines in glass,
absorbed in the precision of his work,
stopping only to run
the black soil through his hands.
I tend to the garden,
pick daffodils and jonquils
to brighten up the kitchen.

And tonight, when the boys are asleep,
John and I will go down to the creek
and wash the day's toils from each other.

THERE'S NO BEAUTY IN BLUE TODAY

Mary, August 1862, when John leaves for war.

There's no beauty in blue today.
Only darkness in this August sky.
But I'll not cry while you're away.

Summer has turned to winter's grey.
Cornflowers are dull to my eye.
There's no beauty in blue today.

You march to end slavery's sway;
a noble cause for which you fight.
But I'll not cry while you're away.

I tell you that I wish you'd stay.
That you must fight is your reply.
There's no beauty in blue today.

For safe return from war, I'll pray;
that soon beside me you will lie.
But I'll not cry while you're away.

Be strong for our young sons, you say,
with one last look into my eyes.
There's no beauty in blue today.
I will not cry while you're away.

ON THIS COLD SOUTHERN FIELD

*Battle of Prairie Grove, Arkansas, December 7, 1862. The battle
lasted until nightfall; many of the wounded, including John, were left
on the field that night.*

Mary,
I lie upon the cold, hard ground,
December stars above this Southern field,
the same as those you see
above our fields in Kansas.
This night is cold and I need warmth.
Shrapnel has pierced my chest and hip,
cutting like the winter wind
that blows across the prairie.

Mary, in the silence of this night
I see your tears as I rode off to war,
leaving you with our boys
and the farm to run.
You did not want me to go.
You questioned the need for war.
But, we came to Kansas to make it free,
and it was now time to free the slaves.

I had no illusions about war.
I knew there would be violence and death.
But, I did not expect such guilt and remorse
from taking another man's life,
from watching others die.
I did not expect the hole
that war would leave in my heart.

Mary, I am cold
and I fear December's stars will fade
before I feel your warmth again.
The air cuts me like a plow through Kansas sod,
slow, ripping at the roots, the black soil
the color of my melancholy soul.

INTO YOUR LOVING CARE
Will Blackburn, 13th Kansas Infantry, Springfield, Missouri, February 1863

Dear Mary,
It is with a heavy heart that I write
to tell you John was gravely wounded.
He was struck by shrapnel in the chest
and a bullet in the hip, then trampled
when the rebel cavalry charged.
The doctors at the hospital here
have done all that they can.
I attended to John as well,
but there is nothing more to do.
We do not think he will live
and are sending him home to spend
his final days with you and the boys.

I wish I had better news to send.
Perhaps if we'd been able
to take him from the field
soon after the fighting ceased
he might have fared better.

War is a terrible thing, Mary.
In all my years of doctoring
I have seen injury, disease, and death,
but I was not prepared for this.
I weep when I see bodies on the field
and wonder if we have forsaken God.

Oh, how I will miss my friend.
I will cherish fond memories
of fishing with John in Ohio
and hunting with him on the prairie.
I will remember how nervous he was
when we came to your uncle's surgery—
John made me pretend I had
medical questions for Thomas,
but he really just wanted to see you.

I fear that I've seen the last of John,
but if anyone can nurse him back to health, it is you.
I pray that in your loving care
my friend can be restored.

I CANNOT FIND BEAUTY
John, Marshall County, Kansas, 1863

I see the signs of spring.
Birds have returned
or are passing overhead, flying north.
Flowers are in bloom,
and buds have appeared on the fruit trees.
But I cannot shake this winter.
Though the days grow longer,
I live in darkness.
Though I am home,
the storm of war surrounds me.

I cannot find the beauty
in the blossoms and the buds.
In the singing of the birds,
I hear only the cries
of the wounded and the dying.
The boys clattering through the house
sound like brigades rushing to battle.
Every clang of a pot or pan unnerves me.

Only in the depths of night,
when all is still, do I find peace.
There are days I wish I'd died on that battlefield.
Then there would have been only one death,
instead of the pain from my wounds
and the daily deaths I endure.

WE WILL WORK THIS FARM TOGETHER

Mary, to her oldest son, Gene, age 12. Spring, 1863

We can do this, Gene.
Your father and I have planted many crops together
in the years we've had this farm,
and you have helped enough
to know what to do.
You harness the horse,
while I check on father.
His wounds are still healing,
but he should be able to watch the baby
(if I can get him to rise from bed—
he's in such a dark mood these days).
John and Fremont can help him,
or they can play in the field while we plow.
With most of the men away at war,
there aren't many around to help,
so we must plow the fields
and then do the planting.
You and I will work this farm together.

WHEN NIGHT COMES, I AM AFRAID TO GO TO BED

Memories of war haunt visceral dreams.
The dead and dying cry out for me,
I lie, bleeding, among them.
It is cold, always freezing cold;
we claw the ground in search of warmth.
Only my scream provides release.

Mary holds me, strokes my head,
tells me to go back to sleep,
but I dare not. Death is always there
to lead me onto shadowed fields
where stretcher bearers wait for me.

I have not slept well for weeks.
This is a fearful fix to be in.

DARKNESS OVER ALL THAT WE HAVE GROWN
John, 1870

The corn is tall and green.
The wheat, tassled and golden.
Apples are ripening to red.
Our fields are full and ready to harvest.

We've settled into a pattern
that seems to suit us well.
Mary and Gene manage the farm.
John helps them in the fields.
My hunting and trapping
fill our smokehouse with meat
and bring money to pay the hired girl
who helps keep the house
and watches after the younger boys.

And, yet, darkness has returned.
I see clouds gathering over the prairie,
storms threatening to flatten
all that we have grown,
and I don't know how to stop them.

GONE AGAIN

John thought he was slipping away,
but I heard every sound
after he got up from the bed.
If he wanted to sneak off
he should have fixed
those creaky floorboards.
I could hear him moving
around the house in the dark—
unsteady, his hip and back
must be bothering him again.
I heard him take his rifle
from its place in the rack,
and then go out to the barn
to hitch his horse to the wagon.

Did he think I wouldn't suspect he'd leave?
He's been silent and distant all week,
staring off across the room,
not listening to the talk at meals.
So many times since the war.
When he gets this way,
it's no use trying to stop him.

I wonder, though,
will he use his rifle only for hunting?
How many days before I must decide
whether to go look for him?

THERE IS LIGHTNESS IN HER STEP
John, 1873

How beautiful she is,
young and slender,
her brown hair pulled back
from her unlined face,
the soft, white skin of her neck
showing above the collar of her dress.

Since Melissa came to work for us
I look forward to each day.
As she moves about the house,
or among the rows in the garden,
there is lightness in her step—
a lightness I have not felt
since returning from the war.
When I am around her,
I feel the stirring of an able man,
not the broken one I've become.

I'VE SEEN THE LOOK IN HER EYES

I know you cannot work as you once did.
I know your old wounds still cause you pain,
but you seem well enough
to spend days hunting and fishing.
Tell me, why do your trips
always end mid-morning?
I know you return to the house
after the younger boys have gone to school,
when I am in the fields with Gene and John,
and only the hired girl is there.
Do you share your thoughts with her?
Why not with me, your own wife?

I've seen the look in her eyes,
the glances exchanged between you two.
Tell me the reason you stop first at the house
is to rest and ease your pain.
Tell me you would rather be in the fields with me,
that you would rather work beside me if you could.

I CANNOT TELL YOU WHAT YOU WANT
TO HEAR

Before we came to Kansas
I worked with my hands
cutting and etching glass,
making objects of beauty.
Working this farm was like that—
straight lines plowed into the ground,
symmetry blending to beauty as crops grew.
The war took all that from me.
I cannot work the fields.
You don't need me to sow the wheat,
plant the corn, tend the stock.

I don't need you to fix me.
The quiet of the prairie,
days spent hunting and fishing,
nights on the prairie with nothing
but the stars and a fire for warmth—
that is all I want and need.

Melissa does not try to fix me.
She does not mind if I sit
in silence and watch her work.
She is never too tired to listen
to me talk about my days on the prairie.
And, didn't I tell you
that I've been teaching her
how to read and write?

Mary, I love you,
but I cannot tell you
what you want to hear.

THE HIRED GIRL
Melissa Hendricks, 1873

I hope Mr. John returns today.
He went hunting on the prairie.
Been gone a week—longer than usual—
but I don't dare say too much about that
or Miz Mary will snap at me
like she did the other day
when I asked when he'd return.
She said she doesn't understand
what's going through his head,
why he can't help more with the farm,
but she knows his wounds weakened him.

I've missed him much this week.
Talking with Mr. John makes the day go by.
He tells me what he's seen on his trips.
We talk about wildflowers and prairie grass,
about how much of the prairie has been plowed up
since he and Miz Mary settled here.
I know all the flowers and trees here in Kansas,
so I ask him about the plants back East.
And the way he talks about the green mountains—
I'd love to see them some day.

Sometimes Mr. John reads to me while I work.
He knows I have a hard time reading,
that sometimes I mix up the letters
and the words don't make any sense.
He's teaching me to write.

Sometimes Mr. John just sits at the kitchen table
and drinks his coffee while I work.
I like that he watches me.
He said I'm pretty—no one's ever told me that.
He seems different when he's with me;
he stands a little straighter
and his face is not so hard.

I hope Mr. John returns today.
If he's not too sore and tired,
we can work together in the garden.
Or, maybe we can just be together in the house.

PERHAPS IT WAS LOVE

Her presence in the house was like dawn
after the night that descended upon him,
the deep depression that drew
every ounce of energy from him.

She was a gentle breeze
across the prairie after the storms
that twisted in his mind.

He did not want to return
to the days when she was not there
working in the kitchen.

Perhaps it was love. Perhaps it was lust.
He could not say, and he did not care.
She made him feel alive again.

AND NOW HE KNEW

He leaned in close to help her form
the letters of the words
he was teaching her to write.
Smell of rosewater and lavender.
His hand over hers, he gently guided.
Mary's in the far field with Gene and John.
Hours before the younger boys come home from school.
They did not complete the line.
Without words, they moved from the kitchen.

He had wondered what it would be like
to lie with her, to hold her body close
cradling her in his arm,
her head resting on his shoulder,
her dark hair loose over her breasts,
her arm across his chest,
her soft skin against his.

She traced her finger
along the scar on his chest
and asked if it hurt him much.
Rain beat a cadence on the roof,
played across the window.
There'll be no more fieldwork in this rain.
He shook his head no,
and knew that this was real.

THE GLASS
Mary, 1873

What happens now that passion's gone,
now that love has flown
like summer before the winter wind?
The cornflower sky is lost to winter's gray;
the cornstalks stand withered in the field,
and even the crows have fled.

Where is the passion you once held
for love, for life… for me?
You are here, but your soul is gone,
left long ago on that battlefield.
I cannot live with your winter and despair;
the lonely days with you;
soundless weeks, followed by sudden gales of anger,
and the terrible hurt that you have caused.

I want summer again,
sunlight and blue skies
and the greening of new fields.

I take from the shelf
the glass you made for me,
hold it to my lips
and take one last sip of emptiness.

As I walk through the door
sunlight breaks the winter clouds
and glints across the sharded floor.

WHEN FREMONT LEFT THE FARM
Gene Ratcliff, 1874

We knew the day would come
when the darkness that troubled Father
would become too much for Mother to bear.

Father had another of his spells,
then, without word, was gone for days.
When he returned, silence hung heavy
as the air before a summer storm.
Tension built like thunderheads over the prairie,
then released in a storm of words
between him and Mother.
John and I took our younger brothers
out to the shelter of the barn.
Fremont fetched his bag;
said it was time to move to town.

I don't blame Fremont for leaving.
I would've left, and John too,
except Mother needed our help on the farm
especially after she told Father to leave.

I see Fremont when I go into town.
He says he doesn't miss the farm.
I told him it's calmer now that Father's gone.
But it's different, too—
like corn stalks flattened after a storm.

THE WHEAT FIELD

Mary, Smith County, Kansas, 1877

Look at you now, broken and bitter,
no spark of the free-soil radical
who, "Beecher Bible" in hand, led us here.
Your dark eyes that once burned with life
now see only shadows.

When you went to war to free the slaves,
grand on your horse like the other men,
you said you'd be fine, and I cried.
You said you'd come home soon,
but you came home changed.
The pain from your wounds paled
to the pain in your heart,
and as the years went by
you sank into darkness,
forsook the vows you made to me,
and I decided I was done with you.

Look at me, sunburnt and hard
from years working our farm.
Here I am, pushing my plow
on my quarter section of western Kansas.
The boys rarely speak of you.
This is our life now,
amid the cottonwoods and the shallow creeks.
And you, alone in your bitter world.
Gene and John said they'll look in on you.

But don't come here and darken my world,
for I plan to turn this prairie green.

JOHN'S LAMENT[1]
Jewell County, Kansas, 1877

Loneliness, thy name is prairie.
The sea of grass brings waves of pain;
tides of guilt wash over me
across the horizons of empty days
and through the endless nights
as long and dark as my despair.

My wounded soul cries into the wind
as it howls across these plains.
I cry alone, lost in my loss of you.
Thoughts of you flood my mind—
your touch, your voice, your love—
but these are just illusions
flashing through the arid night
like streams that rise and then go dry.

Each night builds upon the other,
each darker than the last.
The wind blows harder
against ever-weakening walls,
and builds until it twists the air,
funneling explosive emotions:
memories of war and death and blood;
my black moods,
my betrayal of our love,
the pain that tore us apart,
and the day you told me to leave.

Dawn slips in round shuttered windows.
In the plowed fields laid raw and bare,
I see the faint green shoots of tender wheat.

[1]The first line of this poem is paraphrased from William A. Quayle, *The Prairie and the Sea* (1903): "Loneliness, thy other name, thy one true synonym, is prairie." Quoted in William Least Heat-Moon, *PrairyErth*.

SHE WILL NOT THIRST AGAIN

*John and Mary, Smith County, Kansas, 1882, just before
Mary's death.*

He sits beside her bed,
a prairie of silence between them,
watching her as she sleeps,
gray-streaked hair down,
loose across her shoulders
(the way he always liked it)
framing her face, tanned even in winter.

He has overcome distance,
but cannot conquer time.
The space of years bears the silence;
the words he wanted to say
carried off by the prairie wind
during the ride to her house.
He is glad she sleeps.

He takes a glass from his pocket
and places it on the table next to her bed.
Once one of a pair; now alone,
the other broken years ago.

So he sits, watching, while she sleeps.
With each faltering breath of hers,
and each expectant breath of his,
the silence deepens and closes
the space between them.
Time stops in the fading afternoon.
They are together again.

The sons arrive at her door to break the silence.
Pa, it's time to go. We'll take you home.

The fading sun glints off the glass
and casts a pale blue light across her face.
She will not thirst again.

Additional Acknowledgments

Special thanks go to family, friends, and fellow Baltimore- and Annapolis-area poets whose comments and encouragement helped shape this book, in particular: my sister, fellow writer, and favorite copy editor, Amy Ratcliffe, who touched each poem in this volume in some small or large way; the members of the Savage (Maryland) Writers Group; fellow family historians, Barbara Lee Ratcliffe Collins and Sandra Ratcliffe Compton; Laura Ryan, for agreeing to create the cover art; my parents, Roger and Nelda Ratcliffe; and, of course, my wife, Kathy, and sons, Zach, Dylan, and Harrison.

Bibliographic Note

These poems draw primarily on information contained within John Ratcliff's Civil War Pension File as well as divorce papers filed in the Marshall County (Kansas) Courthouse, and family lore. Other sources that provided inspiration and background information include:

Cutler, William G. *History of the State of Kansas.* 1883. Available on-line at http://www.kancoll.org/books/cutler/ (last accessed March 14, 2015)
Heat-Moon, William Least. *PrairyErth.* 1991. Houghton Mifflin.
Schiller, George W. *The Abolitionist.* 2002. Available on-line at http://www.kancoll.org/books/schiller2/gws_main.htm#contents (last accessed March 14, 2015)

Michael Ratcliffe was born in New Jersey, raised in Maryland, and has roots in Kansas. His poems have appeared in a variety of print and on-line journals, including *Free State Review, The Copperfield Review, Little Patuxent Review,* and *Poetry Quarterly*. When he is not writing poetry, he can be found bicycling around central Maryland, managing census geographic programs, or puttering in his garden. He lives in North Laurel, Maryland with his wife and three sons.